TRUST.

What religions don't tell you
but God wants you to know

by Gordon A. Dickson

ISBN 979-8-9900397-1-1

Live, Serve, Lead, helping others succeed

LiveServeLead.com

Dedication

This book is dedicated to the faculty and staff of Pensacola Christian School who labored fervently to help my classmates and me to understand the good news of Jesus Christ.

Table of Contents

WHY?

Have you ever wished that you could have a conversation with God? If you could talk to Him, what would you ask Him? Most people would ask,

"WHY?"
"Why am I here?"
"Why are things the way they are?"

Even little children learn to ask the "why questions."

Adults ask, "Why is the world so messed up and stressed out with hatred and bitterness?"

Some people ask "why" questions out of misery or frustration. Others ask "why" when they are trying to find real meaning. Would you be surprised to learn that the Bible includes a number of stories about people asking, "Why?"

For instance, Job was so frustrated with his life that he asked, *"Why died I not from the womb? Why did I not give up the ghost when I came out of the belly?"*[1] It sounds as if his life was pretty troubled, doesn't it?

Rebekah was shocked to learn that one of her two sons wanted to murder the other one! She exclaimed, *"Why should I be deprived also of you both in one day?"*[2] Those who have lost children to senseless violence are still asking why they have been deprived of their sons and daughters.

Even Jesus exclaimed, *"My God, my God, why hast thou forsaken me?"*[3]

---

[1] Job 3:11   [2] Genesis 27:45   [3] Matthew 27:46, quoting Psalm 22:1

Across the ages, so many have voiced these questions and others:

"Why are all these painful things happening to me and to the people I love?"

"Why do people say that God loves us when He allows so many harsh and evil things to happen in this world?"

Or "Why do people say that God is in control when it looks as if everything is falling apart?"

Over the years, I have had many conversations with people who asked questions like these. Beginning late in 1971, the Lord began to answer these questions for me. I'm guessing that you wonder about these things as I did and I am eager to share what the Lord has taught me so far. In fact, I am convinced that God put these "Why?" questions into our hearts to help us find our way.

Someone shared this book with you or it came to you by some other means as you ponder the question, "Why?" And this was no accident: the Lord longs to have that conversation with you to explain "Why."

Is There Any Real Meaning?

Are you wrestling through the painful "Why?" questions mentioned in the introduction to this book? Some people say that our struggles and conflicts with harsh realities are only imaginary. Someone even said that the two greatest problems we face are ignorance and apathy—but who knows and who cares? But seriously, why do we think that there is supposed to be meaning behind all the miseries that we face?

There is something inside each of us that tells us there ought to be meaning. We know this deep down in our hearts. It is so obvious that one author put it this way: those who deny that there is meaning are like fish out of water that deny there is any such thing as water. Here is what is happening to you: there are a few witnesses telling your heart that genuine meaning can be found. Would you like to meet them?

You're Surrounded!

This is the reality of living here on earth: people recognize that meaning is missing. Whether they will admit it or not, their surroundings—the earth, human life, wildlife, plant life and the heavens above—are testifying to them. Romans 1:20 explains why this is true: *"For the invisible things of Him [God] from the creation of the world are clearly seen, being understood by the things that are made, even His eternal power and Godhead; so that they are without excuse:"* The visible things around us tell us a great deal about the invisible things that we cannot see with our eyes. Nature, in all its complexity, is telling you about its Maker. This communication is so clear that none of us have an excuse for ignoring this deeper meaning.

9

So why doesn't everyone admit what all of us are seeing? Romans 1:18 answers that question: *"For the wrath of God is revealed from heaven against all ungodliness and unrighteousness of men, who hold [down] the truth in unrighteousness."* The Scriptures testify that every human being can see this meaning in the world around them, but most suppress this truth because it is too painful to admit that it is true. The God who is far above all things has given you this witness to His eternal, powerful existence; all of nature testifies to you each day of your life in a manner that you can understand. We will talk more about that later in this book, but for now, let's talk about the second witness.

Your Conversation with Your Conscience

The second witness that is testifying within each human being is called your "conscience." Where does that come from? If we are just physical beings with no spiritual part, why do we have a conscience? Random clusters of cells don't have a conscience and even complex organs don't grow one. Yet every person on earth has this inner voice called "the conscience." Nations even make laws based on the collective consciences of their people. Romans 2:14–16 explains where your conscience came from and what it does. These verses tell us about what is happening inside each one of us: *"the work of the law written in their hearts, their conscience also bearing witness, and their thoughts the meanwhile accusing or else excusing one another. In the day when God shall judge the secrets of men by Jesus Christ according to my gospel."*[4]

These verses raise all kinds of questions that we will talk about in this book. They tell us about a conversation that each one of us is already having within himself or herself: our thoughts are accusing or excusing us. And those thoughts are a continual reminder that we will one day give an account before God, our Judge.

How does your conscience work? These verses tell you that your conscience *refers you* to an ingrained, inward law that God

---

[4] Romans 2;15–16

has written in your heart. It tells you what it believes to be right and wrong. Not only that, but your conscience *records* the thoughts of your heart and *responds* or talks back to you using that inward law. Your conscience uses your memories to testify to you about the real meaning of things. But most importantly, the human conscience *reminds* each of us to seek to use good judgment knowing that, one day, we will all stand before God, the Judge of all secrets.

So God, who is far above all, testifies to us through His creation (Nature) that surrounds us. But He has also placed a witness deep within each one of our hearts: the conscience. This is the reality about evil and its consequences: our consciences testify to us that this is not the way things ought to be.

Years ago, I was discussing these things with a fellow passenger on a flight. As we talked, he insisted that the concept of evil is merely made-up.

He said, "Evil is just what one religion calls another religion."

I suggested, "When we land, let's change our tickets and fly to South America to find out what the cannibals are having for supper tonight."

He blurted out, "What those people are doing is just wrong!"

"Wait!" I said. "If evil is just what one religion calls another, then who are you to say that they are doing wrong?"

He thought for a moment and then replied, "Well I guess that's right." And then he repeated, "After all, evil is just what one religion calls another."

I looked him in the eye and said, "Let me ask it this way. Are there things that you believe are evil and not because someone told you so? And those things that you believe are wrong, do you go ahead and do them anyway?"

He gave me a wide-eyed look of shock as if to say, "How did you know?"

I continued, "The fact is that our consciences have spoken to our hearts about this evil. And here is one of the ways that you will see that the Bible is true: as you read it, it reads you. It tells you the truth; the Bible can open your eyes to reality. It will tell you what you are really like in a way that confirms the truth your conscience has been telling you all along."

In our search for meaning, we are ably advised by nature around us and our consciences within us. God's creation testifies to you about what is really going on in the universe; your conscience testifies about what is really going on in you. By the way, in addition to the creation and your conscience, there is a third witness, that we will talk about later in this book.

So, how would you like to have a conversation with God? This might surprise you, but He welcomes the opportunity to discuss things with you. As the Lord said in Isaiah 1:18,

"Come now, and let us reason together, saith the Lord: though your sins be as scarlet, they shall be as white as snow; though they be red like crimson, they shall be as wool."

This is a fascinating invitation. Will you accept it? God wants to talk with you in an understandable and rational manner. He wants to talk to you about your problem with evil and the solution that He alone can provide. But how can anyone have this conversation with God? How do we find the deeper meaning behind all these things? Is there any place we can turn to for genuine answers to these questions?

The Bible is full of answers to the "Why?" questions. We are not the first generation of people to ask about the real meaning of things, and we may not be the last. Everyone wants to know, "Why?"

Twisting, Trying or Trusting?

It's important to bear in mind that we all have a tendency to ignore or deny the truth (as we learned earlier in Romans 1:18). Historically, there have been three different responses to God's truth. We can express these in three words: TWIST, TRY or TRUST.

Twist—This is what many people do: they twist the truth. They say that evil is only imaginary or that God is not paying attention to us. They deny what our consciences are telling us. Or they say that a loving God can't possibly mean what He says in His Word. According to Romans 1:18–20, people do this to avoid the devastating realization that they have no excuse for ignoring the living God who loves us.

Try—This is what even more people do. When they begin to understand God's righteous standard, they try to comply. They do so in their own strength, assuming that they have what it takes to be as good as God. Almost all of the religions of the world are about trying to do things to get close to God, but that is not what the Bible is about. God's Word guides you to the third choice:

Trust—This is where the Bible will lead you to—learning where and how to place your faith in what God has promised you is true. As it says in Romans 10:17, *"So then faith cometh by hearing and hearing by the Word of God."*

Believe it or not, the religious leaders of Jesus' time wanted to kill Him because He told them the truth. (You can read about this for yourself in John chapter 7.) They wanted to twist the truth for their own purposes. Why? It was because they had been teaching a religion of "try to comply." And their teaching left the people empty and without hope.[5] They even used some verses from the Bible to

---

[5] See Matthew 23:1–11

try to control the people. But Jesus taught those leaders and the people around Him how to trust. He said, *"If any man will do His will, he shall know of the doctrine [teaching], whether it be of God, or whether I speak of myself"* (John 7:17). Jesus was teaching us all about why and how to approach God as He reasons with us about this earthly life, evil and eternity. If you find your "why" you will find your way.

So bear this in mind as you seek to have your talk with the Lord. You might be tempted to *twist* what He says, or *try to comply* in your own selfish way. But if you will humbly listen to Him, He will lead you to *trust* Him. In Psalm 119:18, King David asked the Lord to open his eyes so that he could behold wonderful things out of God's law. Before you read on, why not ask the Lord to do the same thing for you?

G.R.A.C.E.

What is the Bible about? The Apostle Paul called the Scriptures *"the Word of His grace,"* referring to the glorious message of God's gracious favor toward mankind.[6] He explained that the Bible is able to set you apart, build you up and give you an inheritance that will last forever! In simple terms, the Bible tells you what is right, what is wrong, how to make it right and how to keep it right.[7]

The Gospel (a word meaning "good news") is called *"the Gospel of the grace of God."*[8] This refers to the good news of *how* God extends His gracious favor to men, women, boys and girls. The Gospel of the grace of God is so important that there are people who joyfully give their lives to sharing it with others. It may be that one of those people gave you this book to help you.

So what is the connection between the Bible, *"the Word of His Grace"* and *"the Gospel of the grace of God?"* Here is a way to think about that question: What is the Bible about, and what is the Gospel about? Here is an acronym that will help: G.R.A.C.E.

G—The Glory of God. From cover to cover, the Bible is about the unique excellence of the true and living God. In the next chapter, we will explore more of what that means. This is also where the good news of the Gospel begins: God is glorious. But if God is holy, righteous and gracious, then how did this world get into such a mess? The answer lies in the next letter: "R."

R—The Rebellion of Mankind against God. The Word of God's grace tells us the truth about ourselves. It describes mankind as rebellious, protesting against the God who is glorious. It may not

---

[6] Acts 20:32   [7] 2 Timothy 3:16   [8] Acts 20:24

sound like good news at first, but the Gospel turns on the spotlight to show men how to turn from their rebellion.

But so what? What is the big deal with this rebellion? Aren't people just trying to live their own way? What is the problem with that? Here is the problem:

A—The Awful Penalty for Man's Rebellion against God. It is a big deal. This is why the world is so messed up. God had given men dominion over the earth, but they rebelled against their Creator.[9] When mankind rebelled, the physical world began to rebel against him, just as mankind had rebelled against God. Earthquakes, volcanoes, storms, floods and fires remind us that the earth is groaning under the evil darkness of man's rebellion.[10] But it's not just what is going on across the land; what is going on in our lives is far worse. Why are the consequences for this rebellion such a big deal? They are, quite literally, matters of life and death. Romans 5:12 tells us that it was sin that unleashed death and despair into this world. We will talk more about this rebellion and the penalty for rebellion in upcoming chapters.

C—Christ Paid the Penalty for Man's Rebellion against God. The glory—the unique excellence—of the true and living God is most clearly seen through the Messiah (another word for "Christ") and God's promises about Him. Beginning with His promise in the first book of the Bible and blossoming to ultimate fulfillment in the last book of the Bible, God's distinctive wonders are on full display in Christ. All of the Scriptures point to clear-cut promises about God's Messiah that everyone ought to embrace. The Bible teaches us to *trust* God's promises in Christ to turn us to Him; this is the opposite of religious views that *twist* the truth or insist that men should *try to comply* by making promises to God.

E—Embrace Christ by Faith Today. Every portion of the Bible is designed to lead you to place greater faith in the promises about Christ.[11] Every preacher or teacher who is true to God's Word will

---

[9] Genesis 1:26; 2:15–17; 3:4–8   [10] Romans 8:22   [11] John 5:39, 2 Corinthians 1:19–20

help you place greater trust in the Lord. By faith, your soul can find a resting place that the glorious God has provided for you.

So **G.R.A.C.E.** is the basic outline for the rest of this book. We will discuss God's glory, man's rebellion, the penalty for that rebellion, the glories of Christ who paid that penalty and the great need to let God work in you by faith (trust). This is no small matter. It determines where you will be for all eternity; it's a matter of life and death. This means that time spent finding out is time well spent. You can be rescued from the penalty for your rebellion if you will trust God instead of trying to escape in your own way. As Ephesians 2:8–9 puts it: *"For by grace are ye saved through faith; and that not of yourselves: it is the gift of God: not of works, lest any man should boast."*

The Glory of God

The Bible and the Gospel are about the majestic glory of the true and living God. What does that mean? God's glory refers to His excellent uniqueness: there is no one like Him. From the first pages of Genesis, where we learn that God created the world, to the last pages of Revelation where we learn about God's wonders for all eternity, the Bible portrays the surpassing splendor of God. As God's prophet Jeremiah declared, *"Forasmuch as there is none like unto Thee, O Lord; Thou art great, and Thy name is great in might. Who would not fear Thee, O King of nations?"* [12]

God's glory refers to the fact that He is "the one and only;" no one else is in His category. To glorify Him is to praise His personal characteristics. How can you see the Lord's unique excellence in and around you?

Seeds, Senses and Stars

You can observe God's glory in many ways, because you are surrounded by witnesses to His creativity. You can see this in the smallest seed, through your own senses, and in the largest star.

I like gardening, so let's take a seed, for instance. When you hold a seed in your hand you have the beginnings of a truly remarkable factory that surpasses anything that man (or artificial intelligence) has ever produced. Under the right conditions, that seed is capable of making its own conveyor belts that search the surrounding soil for what it needs. (We call these conveyor belts "roots.") Soil is made up of air, water, organic matter and mineral matter. As gravity draws rainwater down through the soil, those

---

[12] Jeremiah 10:6–7

plant roots are capable of finding moisture and absorbing the ions the plant needs to grow and thrive. Then, that seed can put up its own solar panels (that we call "leaves.") Those can absorb carbon dioxide from the air and store power from the rays of the Sun. Like a miniature factory, plants turn on a process (that we call "photosynthesis") to reorganize water and carbon to make sugar in the fruits and vegetables we eat. While they are at it, they produce the oxygen we breathe. Every human being and every animal is dependent on the products of simple, powerful seeds. How did it all happen? The first verse in the Bible tells you: *"In the beginning God created the heaven and the earth."*[13] Still today, seeds testify to the unique excellence of the all-powerful God. On the third day of Creation, *"God said, Let the earth bring forth grass, the herb yielding seed, and the fruit tree yielding fruit after his kind, whose seed is in itself, upon the earth: and it was so."*[14] And when you bite into that fruit, you sense even more of God's remarkable craftsmanship.

Your tongue contains between 2,000 and 10,000 taste buds that look a little like funnels. Within each taste bud are sensory cells that look like tiny flower buds. And those sensory cells contain thin hair-like filaments surrounded by fluid. When they come into contact with food, they send a signal to your brain which matches that information with your sense of smell. That is exactly how you taste the wonderful bounty of the earth and know the difference between sweet, savory, salty, bitter and sour. And God made it all for you to enjoy! He also helps you to use what you know about taste to understand what you need to know about Him. This is why the psalmist wrote, *"O taste and see that the LORD is good: blessed is the man that trusteth in Him."*[15] If you understand what taste means, then you can understand what trust means. Years ago, a friend of mine said to me, "If you have ever enjoyed the taste of a buttery biscuit then you have a marvelous idea of how to trust the Lord."

Or consider the human eye. Light enters through the transparent front layer called the cornea. The cornea can be curved to help

---

[13] Genesis 1:1   [14] Genesis 1:11   [15] Psalm 34:8

the eye focus. Some of that light passes on through the pupil and through an inner lens. That lens is curved by tiny muscles and fibers to sharpen your focus when you are watching something. The remarkable retina on the back of your eye is equipped with special photoreceptors that turn that light into electrical signals. Those signals are sent to the brain by way of the optic nerve. Your eye is a marvel of mechanical, hydraulic and chemical engineering. Proverbs 20:12 teaches you to glorify God because you can see: *"The hearing ear and the seeing eye, the Lord hath made even both of them."*

If you are reading or listening to this, you are using God's marvelous creation of sight or hearing at this moment. The psalmist used these abilities to illustrate what to do next: *"Come and see the works of God!"*[16] God is inviting you to behold His glory so that He may reason with you about reality.

Then consider what you can learn as you turn your eyes to behold the stars in the heavens above. We have learned much of what we know about the composition of the Sun, Moon and stars by way of total solar eclipses. The Earth is the only known planet in the universe where such total solar eclipses occur.[17] Our Milky Way galaxy contains between 100 billion and 400 billion stars. (Yes, that is an estimate; it is that difficult to count them all!) If our solar system were placed in the midst of those stars then we would not be able to see much of the universe; our evenings would be only a semi-darkness dominated by the largest stars. However, our solar system is placed in this galaxy in such a way that we can see out through the universe to behold its wonders. Through advances such as the Hubble and James Webb telescopes, we are learning how many more galaxies are out there. Present estimates are that there are hundreds of billions of galaxies, and there may be as many as two trillion. The average galaxy contains 100 million stars![18] So

---

[16] Psalm 66:5

[17] See "What the Hidden Reveals" accessed at https://liveservelead.com/solar-eclipse/. The precise dimensions of the Moon and its exact distance from the Sun make our total solar eclipses possible.

[18] Do the math. That means that there are 200 billion trillion stars in the universe!

what does all this mean? What are we supposed to see when we behold the wonders of the night sky? The psalmist David wrote, *"The heavens declare the glory of God ..."*[19] (Psalm 19:1).

Our universe glorifies God's uniqueness. Was it difficult for the glorious God to create the vast array that we can behold in the night skies? In one of the most interesting understatements in the Bible, Genesis 1:16 tells us, *"And God made two great lights; the greater light to rule the day, and the lesser light to rule the night: He made the stars also."* Pompous mankind would consider it to be a great feat to make even one star. The Most High God made an estimated 200 billion trillion stars and listed them all under a passing comment, *"He made the stars also!"*

But wait, there's more. The all-knowing (omniscient) God calls each of the stars by name as the Bible tells us. *"He telleth the number of the stars; He calleth them all by their names. Great is our Lord, and of great power: His understanding is infinite."*[20]

Missing Your Meaningful Glory

Tiny seeds, our own senses and the stars of heaven are testifying to us about the glory of God. Yet our own souls are telling us that we are missing out. How do we know something is missing? It is because of the glory of God in man. About mankind, the psalmist testified that God had *"crowned him with glory and honor!"*[21] That is what's missing. The Bible tells us about the glory—the unique excellence—of mankind, because we were made by God. Apart from God, the apostle Peter summed up our glory this way: *"...all the glory of man [is] as the flower of grass. The grass withereth, and the flower thereof falleth away:"*[22]

You can test this out for yourself and here's how. Proverbs 25:27 advises, *"It is not good to eat much honey: so for men to search their own glory is not glory."* This proverb helps you use what you know to learn what you may not know. If you eat too much honey, then

---

[19] Psalm 19:1   [20] Psalm 147:4–5   [21] Psalm 8:5. (See also Hebrews 2:6–8.)   [22] 1 Peter 1:24

all that sweetness will give you a feeling of sickness. The same thing is true when you try to live for your own glory—trying to build up your proud self-esteem. Glorifying yourself may seem like a sweet way to live, but it will leave you feeling sick and empty. Years ago, I heard an opera singer testify that after his magnificent performances, he would glory in the standing ovations as audiences applauded. But when the curtain dropped for the last time, he felt empty inside. He was on his way to finding the greatest meaning in life—which is to passionately glorify the Lord with your heart and soul and strength. The God of glory crowned humanity with royal glory and honor. To find real meaning in life, you must find your way back to that God-given glory and honor, and God shows you the way. To comfort his people who were asking the "Why?" questions, the prophet Isaiah wrote, "...*All flesh is grass, and all the goodliness thereof is as the flower of the field ... the grass withereth, the flower fadeth: but the Word of our God shall stand for ever.*"[23] God has given you the Word of His grace to help you find your way back to mankind's God-given glory. He will give you the words to say as you seek to have a conversation with Him.[24]

In a scene in Heaven, the Bible tells us what those around the throne of God are proclaiming about Him: "*Thou art worthy, O Lord, to receive glory and honor and power: for Thou hast created all things, and for Thy pleasure they are and were created.*"[25] Learning to glorify the Lord in this joyful manner will make your life meaningful.

The Ways You Cannot Be Like God

The Bible clearly testifies that the true and living God is all-knowing, all-powerful, eternal, unchanging and is everywhere present at once (or omnipresent). This is His unique excellence. He is the Holy Creator and everything else is His creation. No human being—and no other created being—could ever be like Him in this respect. To try to be like God in these ways is the essence of

---

[23] Isaiah 40:6, 8   [24] See for instance Psalm 66:3–4   [25] Revelation 4:11

proud rebellion. No created being could ever exercise the kind of sovereign control that belongs to God alone.

The Ways You Could Be Like God

But there are other ways in which the Lord desires for you to be like Him. He is the God of truth who is also merciful. He is impartial; He treats each man with equity.[26] He is a loving God who is righteously indignant over sin, but He is also full of grace—undeserved favor—toward sinful people. He is the patient Lord who is full of joy and peaceful harmony. His goodness and gentleness can fill us with meaningful greatness.[27]

The God who made the largest star and the tiniest seed also created your ability to see, hear and think through what is written here. This is the God who is appealing to you, *"Come now, let us reason together."*[28] Can such a God clearly communicate with you?

If you have heard the Christmas story, you will remember that outside the little town of Bethlehem, there were humble shepherds keeping watch over their flocks one night. Suddenly,

"The angel of the Lord came upon them, and the glory of the Lord shone round about them: and they were sore afraid. And the angel said unto them, Fear not: for, behold, I bring you good tidings of great joy, which shall be to all people." (Luke 2:9–10)

Think about that. The Most High God, the Lord of glory, sent His messengers to speak to humble, uneducated shepherds. The angel spoke their language. How was that possible? The Creator who made them knew everything about them, and here is the message the angel gave to them: "Don't be afraid." Why not? The angel had brought them good news of great joy. The birth of Christ was the beginning of the good news of the gospel. And it wasn't just for those shepherds, it was for all people: that's you and me too!

---

[26] Psalm 62:11–12   [27] 2 Samuel 22:36, Psalm 18:35   [28] Isaiah 1:18

Don't Be Afraid

You may have found that all this talk about the glory of God caused you to be afraid. If so, remember what the angel said to the shepherds: *"Fear not."* Why not? It's because there is good news of great joy if you will receive it. What is that news? Well, first we need to talk about the bad news that helps us understand why the good news is the greatest news that has ever been given to mankind.

The young woman who sat in my office was referred to me for a particular reason: she had been flagrantly wicked and committed immorality with multiple partners. Yet she insisted that she saw no problem with this lifestyle.

So I began by asking her, "How would you describe God?"

She answered, "He is a God of grace, love, compassion, mercy and kindness."

I asked her if there were any other characteristics of God that she had in mind.

She once again listed those same characteristics and continued by saying, "Most people don't understand that Jesus was just a nice guy."

"So," I asked, "in your opinion would a 'nice guy' make a whip out of cords and drive greedy merchants out of the Temple?"[29]

"I don't suppose He would," she said quietly.

"In fact, what does that tell you about God?" I asked.

She said slowly, "He gets angry."

Stirred by the Lord's compassion at her perceived change of heart, I asked slowly, "So what do you think He is angry at in your life?"

---

[29] Referring to John 2:15

In the next few moments, she stammered and whispered out a number of her sins.

"So," I asked, "Are we talking about the God who is everywhere present, including right here, right now? The God who has all power, and all knowledge? Is He the God of grace, love, compassion, mercy and kindness who is also righteously indignant toward evil?"

"Yes," she said, and it was clear that in just a few moments of time she had a very different view of her sin. In today's society, which grows increasingly wicked, our greatest need is to understand the glorious unique excellence of the true and living God. Only then will we understand how some very bad news can lead us to the greatest news of all.

The Rebellion of Mankind

The Word of God's grace and the Gospel of grace clearly describe and explain the rebellion of mankind against the glorious God.

Who Is The King?

In Jeremiah 10, the prophet referred to the Lord as the *"King of nations."* But, beginning with Adam and Eve in the Garden of Eden, man rebelled against God.[30] In essence, mankind tried to become "man-king," glorying himself alone.

You can see this question of kingship with something such as stealing.[31] Have you ever stolen anything? God commands you not to steal. But why? Why does God command you not to be a thief? It is because He is a glorious giver and stealing is exactly the opposite of His character. The Bible shows us how to turn away from this rebellion of man: *"Let him that stole steal no more: but rather let him labor, working with his hands the thing which is good, that he may have to give to him that needeth."*[32] To give glory to God, a person must stop stealing, work hard and give to those in need. Now be careful: don't *twist* the meaning (of stealing or giving), and don't *try to comply* with this standard by doing it your own way. You must *trust* God to transform you from a thief into a gracious giver. Now you can see the issue much more clearly. If you have ever told a lie, you know that you fall short of the glory of the God who is truth and tells us the truth.

Exalting Yourself

In a confrontation with Pharaoh, the king of Egypt, Moses made an important point. He was appealing to Pharaoh to let the people of Israel go.

---

[30] Read the story for yourself in Genesis chapter 3. [31] Exodus 20:15 [32] Ephesians 4:28

Pharaoh responded, *"Who is the Lord that I should obey his voice to let Israel go? I know not the Lord, neither will I let Israel go!"*[33]

In a later conversation, Moses told the king that God would demonstrate His mighty power in Egypt in order that God's *"name may be declared throughout all the earth."*[34] Then Moses asked Pharaoh this question: *"As yet exaltest thou thyself against my people, that thou wilt not let them go?"*[35] Do you see the problem of the hard-hearted Pharaoh? He was exalting himself and his own glory instead of glorifying the true and living God.

That exaltation of self is one of the chief forms of rebellion against God. Pharaoh hardened his heart so that he had to learn this lesson the hard way. Don't harden your heart; don't insist on exalting yourself. It's not only wicked, it's also dangerous. As we shall see in a later chapter, Jesus warned self-righteous, self-exalting people, pointing out that their eternal destiny was at stake.

This self-exaltation began with Satan who said, *"I will be like the Most High."*[36] Satan also deceived Adam and Eve with the notion that they could be like gods.[37] So this self-exalting human rebellion has run strong throughout human history. People have thought, "God is just like us!" but they were sadly mistaken.[38]

How to See Yourself the Right Way

One of God's prophets learned this important lesson in the Old Testament. He saw a vision of the Lord in Heaven with the angels around His throne proclaiming, *"Holy, holy, holy, is the Lord of hosts: the whole earth is full of his glory"* (Isaiah 6:3). Then Isaiah wrote something else that is important for all of us to hear:

> *"Then said I, Woe is me! for I am undone; because I am a man of unclean lips, and I dwell in the midst of a people of unclean lips: for mine eyes have seen the King, the Lord of hosts"* (Isaiah 6:5).

---

[33] Exodus 5:2 [34] Exodus 9:16 [35] Exodus 9:16–17 [36] Isaiah 14:13–14 [37] Genesis 3:1–5
[38] See Psalm 50:20–22

When Isaiah saw the glory of God and heard the angels proclaiming God's holiness, the prophet saw his own sinful state clearly. The glory of the Lord gave him a whole new understanding of the real problem in himself and in his society. When he understood God's unique holiness, he clearly saw the rebellion of mankind against the Lord of hosts, the Heavenly King. When we truly understand the glory of the King of the nations, there will be no room for self-exaltation.

God's Glory and the Gospel

How is man's rebellion connected to the gospel, the good news of God's grace? Paul explained that, when it comes to righteousness, there is no difference between people: *"For all have sinned, and come short of the glory of God;"*[36] When any one of us compares himself or herself to the unique excellence of the righteous God, we all come up short. This is the only way you and I can recognize our rebellion against God.

"But wait," you might say, "I'm not really that bad!"

Have you ever read a news story about a serial killer or assassin that included a picture of the murderer? Did you find yourself staring at that picture trying to find some hint of the evil masked by that face? In many cases, you studied that boyish figure or the woman's face and wondered if some mistake had been made. Why? It was because the criminal looked like such a nice person.

"Surely that can't be the correct picture," you might have thought. Yet it was the right picture, and that is the real horror. The same people who seem to be so nice can be so evil and so deadly. Now it's important to remember that the evil in them is the evil in you and me (even if we have not acted in a similar way). As Romans 3:10–11 reminds us, *"As it is written, There is none righteous, no, not one: There is none that understandeth, there is none that seeketh after God."* Now as you read this, if there is something in your heart that says that you do want to seek after

---

[39] Romans 3:23

God, then you are experiencing God's gracious favor toward you. If you find that your heart is warmed by this message, then keep reading, because God has a glorious answer for you.

But I'm Doing My Best!

"But," you may ask, "if someone does his best and tries to live right, wouldn't that be enough?"

Now remember: when you read what God says about man's rebellion, you might be tempted to *twist* that truth, or *try to comply* with it somehow. But the Lord wants you to choose the third option: *trust* Him to lead you to understand how He can redeem rebellious people.

When my wife was just 14 years old, she was wrestling with this problem. She asked her mother, "How will I know when my good deeds outweigh my bad deeds so that I can get to Heaven?"

That's the frustrating question that the *"try to comply"* approach will lead to. Can our good deeds ever outweigh our bad deeds?

When you begin with the glory of God, man's unrighteous rebellion becomes painfully obvious. The prophet Isaiah described the way our good deeds look in the eyes of the Holy God:

> *"But we are all as an unclean thing, and all our righteousnesses are as filthy rags; and we all do fade as a leaf; and our iniquities, like the wind, have taken us away."*[40]

Think about these word pictures. Even our best deeds look like filthy rags in God's sight. What is the result? Our iniquities are driving us along like the winds of fall drive lifeless leaves to skitter along the cold ground. Filthy rags and lifeless leaves: those aren't flattering pictures are they? Yet if we are going to have a conversation with God, we have to start with this understanding.

But how did we get to this place? The apostle Paul listed five phrases or steps, to illustrate how people make a rebellious fist in the face of God. You can illustrate this process for yourself.

---

[40] Isaiah 64:6

Beginning with an open hand, bring one of your fingers down to your palm as you read each of these phrases to make a fist:

> *"Because that, when they knew God, / they glorified him not as God, / neither were thankful;/ but became vain in their imaginations,/ and their foolish heart was darkened"* [41] *(Romans 1:21)*

What happens when people (1) see the light of the glory of God in the creation around them and yet (2) refuse to praise His unique excellence? They also (3) refuse to give Him thanks; and then (4) their thoughts become futile and empty. What is the result? (5) Their foolish hearts are darkened. These five steps to making a fist show us how man became a rebel against God, beginning with Adam and Eve. This is a terrible waste of the glory of God in man; it's how people start living for their nerve endings rather than what is never-ending. Instead of using their bodies as a tool for the Lord's glory, they use their bodies as a toy for their lusts and come away feeling empty and meaningless.

Religious Rebellion

Let's face it: sometimes religious rebellion is just as bad as all the other kinds; horrible atrocities have been committed with religious passion. How did that happen? The apostle Paul wrote,

> *For I bear them record that they have a zeal of God, but not according to knowledge. For they being ignorant of God's righteousness, and going about to establish their own righteousness, have not submitted themselves unto the righteousness of God.* [42]

Paul was describing religious people who decide to *try to comply* with God's righteousness by doing deeds that they think are good. However, the real problem is that they are unwilling to submit to the righteousness of God. They are unwilling to *trust* Him for answers. Is this really a big problem? Yes, and the Bible shows us just how big the problem is.

---

[41] Romans 1:21–32 describes what happens when men and women deny the glories of God that can be seen in nature around them.

[42] Romans 10:2–3

The Awful Penalty for the Rebellion of Mankind

What happened when mankind rebelled against God? It opened up a giant chasm of separation between the righteous God and rebellious man. How can men cross this chasm to get to God?

Picture the Grand Canyon in the western United States. At its widest, the Grand Canyon is 18 miles (29 km) across; but even at its narrowest point it is 4 miles (6 km) across. So how would you respond if someone suggested a running long jump contest to see who could jump across the Grand Canyon? That's crazy isn't it? Yet our own consciences tell us that a chasm of separation exists between God and us because of our sin. That's how we are missing the meaning in life. So what should we do?

We could *twist* our consciences to tell ourselves that there is no chasm of separation. Many people abuse substances in an attempt to forget about the heartaches and horrors brought on by the way their sin has separated them from God. We could *try* to cross this chasm of separation by our own strength—knowing all the while that we will never make it. Or we could *trust* someone else to bridge the gap for us—to bring us to God.

Why do people die? Simply put, *"the wages of sin is death."*[43] The monster that we call "Death" was unleashed upon this world by sin—the rebellion of men against God. Every time you see a hearse on its way to a cemetery, you should think about the curse of sin. Every disease and every disaster is a reminder that *"the wages of sin is death."*

---

[43] Romans 6:23

Death is the separation from life. As the Lord said through His prophet Ezekiel, *"Behold, all souls are mine; as the soul of the father, so also the soul of the son is mine: the soul that sinneth, it shall die."*[44] The awful penalty of death has been passed upon every human being. However, the Lord wasn't just talking about physical death. There is a much more horrifying death—spiritual death!

It is one thing to be physically dead—to be separated from physical life; but it is quite another to be spiritually dead—separated from spiritual life. According to the Bible, from our first moments on earth, each one of us was *"dead in trespasses and sins."*[45] How can you know this is true? When Adam sinned in the Garden of Eden, all mankind inherited a love for sin. Rather than serve the Lord (a relationship rich with meaning), men serve their evil lusts (which they soon learn is meaningless). We were all born loving sin rather than the Savior and this is how a person can know he or she is separated from the Lord and *"dead in trespasses and sins."*

But there is an eternal danger to remaining in that dead state. As the Bible says, *"And as it is appointed unto men once to die, but after this the judgment."*[46] The Bible teaches that you have one life here on earth, followed by a hearing before God, the Judge of all. Your conscience is also warning you about this reality. In fact, every person on earth understands what it means to be one of those *"who through fear of death were all their lifetime subject to bondage."*[47] Imprisoned by fear, thinking people want to avoid the prison of fire. But if you pass into God's presence still spiritually dead, then your punishment will be a never-ending fiery torment. Does the Bible really teach that?

A Terrifying Conversation

Now bear in mind that we are talking about your eternal destiny. Time spent finding out about this is time well-spent. In the Gospel of Luke, chapter 16, Jesus told us about a very wealthy man who died and went to that terrible place of torment called, "Hell."

---

[44] Ezekiel 18:4   [45] Ephesians 2:1   [46] Hebrews 9:27   [47] Hebrews 2:15

From that awful place, he cried out to Abraham whom he could see resting in Paradise. That rich man begged for someone to cross the chasm to that infernal place to give him some relief.

But Abraham responded, *"Between us and you there is a great gulf fixed: so that they which would pass from hence to you cannot; neither can they pass to us that would come from thence."*[48]

There is a separation between God and sinful men that is far greater than the chasm of the Grand Canyon. But if that separation is still in place when a person dies, then he or she will be apart from God for all eternity. That rich man in Hell is personally enduring the awful penalty for his rebellion against God at this moment, and he has been there for more than 2000 years!

"But why is he there?" you might ask.

Think carefully about the rich man's conversation with Abraham. Since he couldn't get relief from his fiery torment, he asked Abraham to send someone to warn his brothers.

He said, *"I pray thee therefore, father, that thou wouldest send him to my father's house: for I have five brethren; that he may testify unto them, lest they also come into this place of torment."*[49]

Let that settle into your thoughts. This is the testimony of a man in Hell. He longs for someone to go warn his family members about that awful place, so that they would not end up there as he had. With an approach like that, you have to wonder why he is in Hell in the first place. The rest of that conversation in Luke 16:29–31 answers our question, "Why?"

In answer to the man's appeal, Abraham responded, *"They have Moses and the prophets; let them hear them."*[50]

By the expression *"Moses and the prophets"* Abraham referred to the Old Testament. (The New Testament had not yet been completed.) Abraham told the rich man that his brothers needed to pay careful attention to the Bible—the Word of His grace. But the

---

[48] Luke 16:26   [49] Luke 16:27–28   [50] Luke 16:29

rich man twisted that truth by denying its power and insisting on something else.

He declared, *"Nay, father Abraham: but if one went unto them from the dead, they will repent."*[51]

Did you get that? The rich man in Hell was still insisting on setting the terms for how someone could avoid Hell! Huh? He insisted on signs or wonders—like someone returning from the dead. Exalting his own understanding, he denied the sufficiency of God's Word of grace to turn someone back to God. This is terrifying! But this same thing is going on in every person who *twists* God's truth or *tries to comply* in his own way. They don't really *trust* God and His Word.

Abraham answered him, *"If they hear not Moses and the prophets, neither will they be persuaded, though one rose from the dead."*[52]

Don't make that rich man's mistake. Trust God that His Word of grace is sufficient to bring you to God.

Who Can Pay for Something That Is Priceless?

Look at the problem this way: how would you pay for something that is priceless? It's pretty difficult to set a value on something that is priceless. So what if we put the question a different way: how would you pay for the most expensive thing in the world?

According to a recent article, the most expensive thing in the world is the History Supreme Yacht which costs just under $5 billion dollars. So let's say that you were on that yacht, sailing across the Marianas Trench (which is 7 miles deep in the Pacific Ocean). Then, through something that you did on board, your actions blew open a gaping hole in the side of the ship and it sank to the bottom of that trench. Then let's say that, after you were rescued, the lawyers for the ship's owner presented you with a bill for $5 billion dollars, payable immediately.

---

[51] Luke 16:30   [52] Luke 16:31

You would say, "I don't have that kind of money!"

The lawyer would respond, "Pay up or find somebody who will!"

Needless to say, your life would be wrecked at that point. Your life's work, including any future earnings, would all be owed to the ship's owner. If the interest rate on that five billion were 5%, then you would owe an additional $65,000 in interest every day until you paid that debt. Each year, you would owe $25 million in interest alone. There are few people on earth who could pay that $5 billion. There are no people on earth who could pay for what is priceless. Yet our sinful rebellion against God has violated His priceless, righteous glory. Now each person has a debt that he or she can't pay. What can we do?

We can attempt to *twist* our consciences to deny that we owe such a debt. We could attempt to *try* to repay that priceless debt. Or we could *trust* someone else who could pay the debt for us. (As the lawyer put it, "Pay up or find somebody who will!") It's time to talk to the One who could pay your priceless debt.

Christ Paid the Penalty for the Rebellion of Mankind

Making an Exchange

More than a decade ago, I sat on a bench in our church hallway with a young man and young woman. Before us were five posters spelling out the G.R.A.C.E. acronym explained in this book. I began by asking them this question, which I would also pose to you:

"If you had to stand before God in His Heaven, and He were to ask you, 'What will you give in exchange for your soul?' what would your answer be?"

The young man immediately responded, "I've been baptized!"

And then he paused to inquire, "Is that the right answer?"

I said, "Let's talk." And over the next several sessions I used those G.R.A.C.E. posters to explain what you are reading in this book.

Jesus invited us all into this important conversation with a puzzling comment and two questions. First, the comment that seems like a contradiction: Jesus said, *"For whosoever will save his life shall lose it: and whosoever will lose his life for my sake shall find it."* [53] With this curious statement, Jesus showed us how people miss out on life; they never find the meaning that they knew they were missing.

Then, with his first question, Jesus framed the issue in commercial terms we could all understand: *"For what is a man profited, if he shall gain the whole world, and lose his own soul?"*

According to Jesus, even if you owned all the material things in the world, you could still miss the real meaning in life

---

[53] Matthew 16:25–26

"Or what shall a man give in exchange for his soul?"

In the last chapter (describing the awful penalty for rebellion), we learned what it could mean to *"lose his own soul."* To apply this pointed question from Jesus, we could ask: "What if you could win by being the richest person on earth, yet lose by being sent to torment for all eternity? Would it be worth it to you?"

The Eternal Exchange Offered to You

God the Father sent God the Son to this earth to address this very question for you and me. The Father did so to show us His glory—His unique excellence. God's Son, Jesus Christ, came to this earth to live the righteous life that every one of us should have lived. Then, in our place, He died the sinner's death that every one of us should have died. Death could imprison us, but death couldn't imprison Jesus.[54] Three days after Jesus was buried, He rose again to show us the unique excellence of the true and living God. The Bible includes eyewitness testimonies to this truly startling event. By rising from the dead, Jesus paved the way; He became our bridge to eternal life. He showed us how to escape our bondage to the fear of death by trusting in Him. Those who trust Christ's sacrificial work—embracing Him by faith—will pass *"from death unto life"* and escape fiery torment in eternity.[55] This is the great exchange: Jesus offers to take your place for He has already paid the price! He offers to take your sin upon himself and to clothe you in His perfect righteousness so that you can enter into Heaven.

Perhaps the most well-known verse in all the Bible makes this clear: *"For God so loved the world, that He gave his only begotten Son, that whosoever believeth in Him should not perish, but have everlasting life"* (John 3:16).

Among all His other glorious characteristics—His truth, His mercy, His righteous indignation toward sin, His justice and grace—God loves us. He sent His Son to this earth with His

---

[54] Note Peter's statement in Acts 2:24 based on eyewitness accounts, Acts 2:32; 3:15.
[55] John 5:24, 1 John 3:14

message of love. When I think of "love" I think of "Living for Others Victory for Eternity:" L.O.V.E. That's what the Father sent His Son to do for us: live for our victory for eternity. We can be *saved by his life*—His record of the sinless life that He lived here on earth.[56]

For His entire ministry, Jesus served in the presence of enemies who watched his every move. One of those who followed Him closely was Judas, who also served as the treasurer for His disciples. If anyone should have been able to find fault with Jesus, it should have been Judas. Yet after he betrayed the Lord, Judas' own conscience compelled him to testify, *"I have sinned in that I have betrayed the innocent blood!"*[57]

Jesus lived perfectly here on earth so that you could live in victory for all eternity. Jesus Christ is the bridge across the eternal chasm that none of us could cross by his or her own power. As the Bible says, *"But God commendeth his love toward us, in that, while we were yet sinners, Christ died for us"*[58] God has demonstrated his L.O.V.E. to you. Though you are a sinner, the Son of God sacrificially gave His perfect life for you. He offers to exchange places with you: Christ's record of His sinless life for your cursed record of rebellious, sinful living. Just as you might graciously make a deposit in someone else's bank account, Jesus offers to place His righteousness on your account. He offers to do so *"that He might bring us to God."* That's the way the apostle Peter described Christ's life-giving exchange for you: *"For Christ also hath once suffered for sins, the just for the unjust, that He might bring us to God, being put to death in the flesh, but quickened by the Spirit."*[59]

I recently met a young man carrying a Bible in a public park. Intrigued, I asked him that same question that I mentioned earlier.

I asked, "If you had to stand before God in His Heaven and He were to ask you, 'What will you give in exchange for your soul?' what would your answer be?"

---

[56] Romans 5:10   [57] Matthew 27:3–4   [58] Romans 5:8   [59] 1 Peter 3:18

"Nothing," he replied.

"Nothing?" I asked, surprised. "Well, if you would offer Him nothing, then how will you deal with your problem of personal evil? Something has to be given in exchange for your soul for you to get to Heaven."

"There is nothing I can give," He answered flatly.

"So, has someone given something for you?" I inquired.

"Yes!" he smiled, and began to tell me about what Jesus Christ had done for his soul. As he talked I could tell he had grasped God's glorious answer to the biggest "Why?" question. Have you?

Your record of good works or baptisms or charitable giving is not a sufficient exchange for your sinful soul. Only the perfect life of Jesus—the exchange of His sinless life for your sinful life—will suffice to redeem you from the curse of sin, death and Hell.

The Warning and the Welcome

The horrible crucifixion of Jesus Christ demonstrated both God's wrath against sin and His gracious mercy for men. That one event communicates both a warning and a welcome. You can't have the welcome without the warning. In a remarkable display, the cruel death of Jesus shows you God's righteous indignation toward your sin; but it also portrays His mercy to you, for Jesus died as your Substitute and Savior. It's essential for each one of us to call upon God for mercy in order to escape eternal miseries. Forty days after Jesus rose from the dead, He ascended into heaven where He was enthroned at the right hand of God the Father. Jesus Christ the Lord will return as the Judge of this world. God the Father has already appointed a day in which Jesus will judge every man. God gave us the assurance of this coming judgment when He raised Jesus from the dead. The One who is the Savior will one day return as our Judge. Remember what we learned in chapter 1: your conscience is telling you about *the day when God shall judge the secrets of men by Jesus Christ according to my gospel.*

This glorious salvation in Christ demonstrates the unique excellence of the true and living God. As the Bible puts it, *"To God only wise, be glory through Jesus Christ forever. Amen."*[60] Jesus proclaimed His unique excellence with these words, *"I am the way, the truth, and the life: no man cometh unto the Father, but by me."*[61] There is no other way of salvation.[62] Jesus is *the* way, not *a* way. In a manner that magnifies the unique excellence of God, this is the one way of salvation. It was only necessary for Jesus to die once to pay for your eternal salvation. As the Bible tells us, *"So Christ was once offered to bear the sins of many; and unto them that look for Him shall He appear the second time without sin unto salvation."*[63] Jesus died that all-sufficient death for you, and He will return to claim His own and rule this world.

Jesus Christ came to this earth and lived the righteous life that every one of us should have lived. Then, in our place, He died the sinner's death that every one of us deserved. Dying on the cross and rising again bodily from the grave, Christ completed His work of righteousness on our behalf. Moments before Jesus died on the cross, He proclaimed, *"It is finished!"*[64] With those words, He communicated the idea of "paid in full" (which a merchant of the time might stamp on a completed transaction).[65] By shedding His blood on the cross, Jesus paid for each believer's eternal redemption fully and completely. His finished work (His death, burial and resurrection) is the only basis for each sinner's salvation. Paul referred to this as *"the light of the glorious gospel of Christ . . . the light of the knowledge of the glory of God in the face of Jesus Christ."*[66]

The Life that Overcomes Death

A difficult "Why?" conversation is recorded in the Bible. A grieving sister named Martha wanted to know why Jesus had not come to heal her brother, Lazarus, before he died. She knew her brother would *"rise again in the resurrection at the last day."*[67] But

---

[60] Romans 16:27   [61] John 14:6   [62] Acts 4:12   [63] Hebrews 9:28   [64] John 19:30
[65] He used the Greek word [*tetelestai*]   [66] 2 Corinthians 4:4–6   [67] John 11:24

she wanted to know why Jesus hadn't made the short journey to heal her brother and keep him from dying a few days earlier.

What happened next was a truly awe-inspiring display of the unique excellence of the true and living God.

Jesus said, "*I am the resurrection, and the life: he that believeth in me, though he were dead, yet shall he live. And whosoever liveth and believeth in me shall never die. Believest thou this?*"[68]

One of the characteristics of God is life—the kind of life that overcomes death forever. The Son of God told Martha that those who would trust Him as the Source of the resurrection and the life would live forever. (Jesus proceeded to confirm His message by performing the miracle of raising Lazarus from the dead!)[69] And He is asking you to trust Him so that you too can take part in His life, which overcomes death. When you do, you will find rest for your soul.[70]

Now you are once again faced with those three choices: Will you *twist* God's truth by insisting that there are many ways to Heaven? Or *twist* the truth so that you can try to proudly add something to Christ's finished work? Or will you *try to comply* with God's righteous standard your own way, insisting that you have to earn this gift that Jesus has already purchased for believers? Or will you *trust* Him for His finished work as the only way to get to Heaven: by grace alone, through faith alone in Christ alone?

---

[68] John 11:25–26   [69] John 11:30–45   [70] Matthew 11:28–29

Embrace Christ by Faith Today

Throughout this book, we have discussed your having a conversation with the Lord. Remember, He is longing to have this conversation with you personally. The Lord made this direct appeal to a nation full of sinful people: *"Come now, and let us reason together, saith the Lord: though your sins be as scarlet, they shall be as white as snow; though they be red like crimson, they shall be as wool."*[71] In the next chapter we will talk about how to begin this conversation sincerely. But now we need to talk about how to embrace Christ by faith today.

We have discussed how rebellious man falls short of the glorious God and faces awful consequences for this rebellion. But Christ paid the penalty for man's rebellion and He freely offers salvation as a gift for those who will humbly repent to turn to Him.

The issues about evil and eternity are very real for all humanity. As the psalmist put it, *"If thou, Lord, shouldest mark iniquities, O Lord, who shall stand? But there is forgiveness with Thee, that thou mayest be feared."*[72] If there were no way to receive forgiveness for sins, then all of us would fall and fail. Before the Lord, we are all sinners (even if we do not consider ourselves to be as great a sinner as someone else). If there were no way of being forgiven, what might we do? We could plead; we could beg; but if there were no way to be forgiven, all that pleading would be in vain. We might look for a way to *twist* the

---

[71] Isaiah 1:18   [72] Psalm 130:3–4

45

painful truth to get it out of our thoughts. Or we could *try to comply* with God's righteous standard, knowing all the while that our sins are like an anchor, ready to plunge us into eternity at any moment. But the psalmist rejoiced, *"But there is forgiveness with Thee that thou mayest be feared!"* In other words, there is a way that rebels can have a respectful relationship with the Lord; but it is only because God grants forgiveness! If you embrace this forgiveness on God's terms, you will find the answer for those accusations from your conscience.

Asking the Lord for Understanding

Earlier in this book, I urged you to pray as David did when He asked the Lord to open his eyes so that he could see wonderful things in God's Word.[73] The fact that you are still reading is encouraging. If you sense that God is giving you light, ask Him for more.

The Bible described this enlightenment in a fascinating way: *"For God, who commanded the light to shine out of darkness, hath shined in our hearts, to give the light of the knowledge of the glory of God in the face of Jesus Christ."*[74] Just as God said, *"Let there be light, and there was light,"* at Creation, so God can command His light to shine in your heart right now.[75] Ask Him to command His light to shine in your heart.

Long ago, in the city of Philippi, a religious woman named Lydia attended a riverside worship meeting. As she listened to the preaching of the Apostle Paul, something wonderful happened to her. The Bible tells us about Lydia, *"whose heart the Lord opened that she attended unto the things which were spoken of Paul."*[76] Why not ask the Lord to open your heart the same way?

---

[73] Psalm 119:18   [74] 2 Corinthians 4:6   [75] Genesis 1:3   [76] Acts 16:14

Giving Glory to God

Throughout this little book, we have talked about giving glory to God. His excellent uniqueness is worthy of all our praise. But now we come to the essential way to apply what we have been discussing: *trust.* Embracing Christ by faith means that you glorify God's uniqueness by accepting Christ's payment for sin as the only way that He offers you salvation. The Bible describes this as the life-changing point at which people *"turned to God from idols to serve the living and true God."* [77] This is what Jesus meant when He commanded, *"Repent for the kingdom of heaven is at hand!"* [78] It's time to turn to the true and living God and away from what is false. You can embrace Christ today by humbly believing and depending upon God's promises to you.

A passage in Romans chapter four is very enlightening on how to do this. Referring to a story in the Old Testament, it tells us how Abraham placed his faith in God, giving glory to Him; you can too. In these verses, you will see the word "imputed," which we don't often use nowadays. The word means "to place something on an account." These verses tell us how God placed eternal righteousness on Abraham's account!

> *[Abraham] staggered not at the promise of God through unbelief; but was strong in faith, giving glory to God, and being fully persuaded that, what [God] had promised, He was able also to perform. And therefore it was imputed to [Abraham] for righteousness. Now it was not written for his sake alone, that it was imputed to him; but for us also, to whom it shall be imputed, if we believe on Him that raised up Jesus our Lord from the dead; who was delivered for our offenses, and was raised again for our justification.* [79]

(The word "justification" means to be declared righteous in God's sight.)

---

[77] 1 Thessalonians 1:9   [78] Matthew 4:17   [79] Romans 4:20–25

This passage is packed with God's splendor, but it also practically guides us in how to embrace Christ as Savior. When Abraham and Sarah were about 75 years of age, they were childless.[80] Yet shortly after they moved to Canaan (modern day Israel), God promised Abraham that they would have a child and inherit what came to be called "The Promised Land."[81] And one of the promises that God gave to Abraham is the most significant promise in the history of mankind!

God promised, *"in thee shall all families of the earth be blessed."*[82] To be very specific, the Lord later explained that promise by saying, *"And in thy seed shall all the nations of the earth be blessed; because thou hast obeyed my voice."*[83] This "seed" or descendant of Abraham is a reference to Jesus Christ, God's Son who would become a man on earth.[84] Why is this blessing so significant? After Jesus died and rose from the dead, the apostle Peter described the blessing this way: *"Unto you first, God, having raised up his Son Jesus, sent Him to bless you, in turning away every one of you from his iniquities."*[85] By this blessing from the Lord you can find real meaning in life.

Now here is the point about faith: even though Abraham and Sarah were 75 years old, the Lord promised them that they would bear a child. That sounds impossible, doesn't it? Yet Abraham chose to place his faith in the Lord's promises—giving God glory. At that moment, the Lord made Abraham a participant in the great exchange. Though Abraham had the record of a sinner, God placed eternal righteousness on his account!

That's amazing! How did it happen? The verses above tell you that Abraham believed in what God had promised. Do you believe that about God? Abraham placed his complete confidence in the Lord, exalting God's unique excellence. Did Abraham and Sarah have a child right away? No! But 25 years later, when they were close to 100 years of age, God gave them a son named Isaac.

---

[80] Genesis 11:30; 12:4   [81] Genesis 12:3–7   [82] Genesis 12:3   [83] Genesis 22:18
[84] See Galatians 3:16   [85] Acts 3:26

Now if you are thinking through this story, you are asking, "How could 75 year-olds, much less 100 year-old olds become parents?"

And the answer is, "Because God had promised." And they believed that what God had promised, He was able to perform.[86]

But remember, this story has personal significance for you. As the Bible explains: *"Now it was not written for [Abraham's] sake alone, that it was imputed to him; but for us also, to whom it shall be imputed, if we believe on Him that raised up Jesus our Lord from the dead; who was delivered for our offenses, and was raised again for our justification."*[87]

Here is the important lesson from Abraham: he glorified God by believing God's promise, even though he didn't know how that was humanly possible. But when Abraham trusted God, the Lord exchanged His righteousness for Abraham's sinful account and gave him eternal life.

Now you and I are called upon to believe God's promise concerning His Son, Jesus. God the Father raised His crucified Son from the dead. Humanly speaking, that sounds impossible, doesn't it? But just as Abraham trusted God to give them a child in old age, you and I must trust that God raised Jesus bodily from the dead. Do you believe this? If you believe in your heart that God raised Him from the dead and confess Jesus Christ as Lord, God has promised to give you eternal life. Here is God's personal promise to you: *"That if thou shalt confess with thy mouth the Lord Jesus, and shalt believe in thine heart that God hath raised him from the dead, thou shalt be saved."*[88] Will you give glory to God at this moment by embracing Christ Jesus as your Lord today?

It's not about a Journey; It's about Jesus

World religions are all about trying to do things to get close to God. But the Bible is about trusting the things that God has done to get close to you. What has God done to get close to you? God

[86] Romans 4:21   [87] Romans 4:23–25   [88] Romans 10:9

loved you so much that He gave His one and only Son for you. All those who place their trust in Him will escape eternal punishment and receive everlasting life. He has given you His promises to assure you that these things are true. Saving faith is not about making promises to God but about trusting the promises from God. Don't *twist*; don't *try*; just *trust*.

Recently I asked a young lady about whether or not she was sure that she was going to Heaven.

She responded, "I'm on a journey," and gave no explanation.

Not long after I became a Christian late in 1971, the leader of our church said something similar to me. He began to ask me some pointed questions about what was going on in my life. After I told him that I had embraced the Lord by faith to become a believer, he said something that startled me.

He said, "Gordon, all of us as we go through life at some time or other are saved."

"Really? Everyone?" I asked earnestly, "So pastor, when were you saved?"

I could tell that my question angered him and he ended the conversation abruptly. That pastor's false teaching reflects what so many people mean when they say they are on a spiritual journey. Be careful! The apostle described some people who are. *"Ever learning, and never able to come to the knowledge of the truth."*[89] Some people encourage you to take such a fruitless spiritual journey which is ultimately meaningless. But would you be surprised to learn that the Bible says exactly the opposite?

The Bible puts it this way:

> *But the righteousness which is of faith speaketh on this wise, "Say not in thine heart, 'Who shall ascend into heaven? (that is, to bring Christ down from above:) Or, who shall descend into the deep? (that is, to bring up Christ again from the*

---

[89] 2 Timothy 3:7

dead.)"' But what saith it? "The word is nigh thee, even in thy mouth, and in thy heart:" that is, the word of faith, which we preach; that if thou shalt confess with thy mouth the Lord Jesus, and shalt believe in thine heart that God hath raised him from the dead, thou shalt be saved. (Romans 10:6–9)

Speculating about whether Christ really came from Heaven is an attempt to *twist* the plain truth from God. Wondering how you might *try* to get to Heaven or find salvation some other way is equally dangerous. The fact is that the Bible clearly teaches that God sent His Son into the world to save sinners. The Lord has given you the Word of His grace in a clear and straightforward manner that speaks directly to your heart. Will you respond to it? It is dangerous to delay. If you read the Bible with an open heart, you will find that it reads you. You can see this for yourself by reading the Gospel of John or the Book of Romans. Ask the Lord to enlighten your heart and He will.

As the verses above tell you, the Word of God's grace is near to you and speaking to your heart. What does it tell you? It tells you how God can turn you away from your rebellion to confess Jesus as your Lord. If you believe that God raised Jesus from the dead, call upon Him now and you will be saved for all eternity! This is His promise. Will you embrace that promise by trusting Him?

A good friend of mine contracted tuberculosis and was sent to a tuberculin hospital in his country, India. There he was surrounded by caring people who were sharing the same message we are discussing here, and it angered him.

He told me, "So I decided to read their Bible so that I could show them how mistaken they were. I read it all the way through to try to master its content. Then, I decided to read it through one more time to be sure I knew what I was talking about. When I finished reading the Bible a second time, I thought, "Ok, one more time through and I will be ready to talk to them."

"What happened next?" I asked.

He smiled. "When I got to Jeremiah 17:9–10, I fell to my knees and called upon the Lord to save me!"

Would you like to know what the Lord said to him through those two verses? Here it is:

The heart is deceitful above all things, and desperately wicked: who can know it? I, the Lord, search the heart, I try the reins, even to give every man according to his ways, and according to the fruit of his doings.

The Bible showed my friend that his heart was deceiving him. That's tough to admit! But those who won't admit that will attempt to *twist* God's truth or *try to comply* in their own way. But who can know when his heart is deceiving him? Only the Lord can show someone that startling truth. God can show you His power over your heart, even as He reminds you that He is the ultimate Judge of all secrets. Those two verses correspond exactly to what your conscience is telling you (as we learned earlier from Romans 2). They tell you how you are missing real meaning in life and where to find it.

Do you believe that God the Father raised up His Son, Jesus, from the dead? If so, you can you have a conversation with Him right now to ask Him to be your Lord, just as my friend did. In His very first message, Jesus said, *"Repent: for the kingdom of heaven is at hand!"* [90] He commanded sinners to turn from their rebellion to embrace Jesus as King and Lord.

Creation, Conscience and the Comforter

In the early pages of this book, we talked about two witnesses who are already testifying to you: creation around you and your conscience within you. But we mentioned that there is a third witness; He is the Holy Spirit, who is also called "the Comforter." [91]

Earlier in the book we talked about the effect of this heart-warming message on you, and encouraged you to keep reading. The

---

[90] Matthew 4:17 [91] John 14:26

Holy Spirit, who does this great work of drawing you to himself, is the Comforter. Keep reading, and He will lead you to a glorious answer to your questions; He will lead you to Christ.

The Spirit of God inspired the Word of His Grace and He is the One who is speaking to your conscience at this moment. He is confronting people all over the world about three significant matters: the reality of sin, the matchless righteousness of Christ and the coming judgment of Satan and all who follow him. [92]

In the next chapter, let's discuss that conversation you need to have with the Lord. But please keep something important in mind. Praying a prayer will not save you; only placing your complete faith in the Lord will save you.

It's Time to Believe and Depend upon the Lord

In 2012, Nik Wallenda walked a tightrope across Niagara Falls, and some reporters said that it was the first time that had ever been done. But they didn't know their history. A man whose stage name was Charles Blondin walked a 1000 foot tightrope over those falls so frequently that Abraham Lincoln used Blondin's performances to illustrate his speeches. Blondin routinely walked that tightrope, 190 feet above the raging torrent. He did it so often that he had to invent ways to make his performances more exciting. On one occasion, he placed a camp stove in a wheelbarrow and stopped to cook himself an omelet as he stood suspended above the falls! One day he rolled a large sack of potatoes across to the other side in that wheelbarrow, and the crowd cheered. As he stepped off the rope, he quieted the crowd to pose a question.

He said, "This sack of potatoes weighs 250 pounds, which is more than most of you weigh. How many of you believe that I could roll you across the tightrope to the other side?"

Quietly at first, but growing ever louder, the crowd began to chant, "I believe! I believe! I believe!"

---

[92] John 16:8–11

So Blondin pointed to a man chanting loudly in the front row and said, "You sir! Please get into my wheelbarrow." The people laughed as the man screamed in fright and ran to the back of the crowd.

That story illustrates the difference between saying that you believe in someone and actually making the commitment to trust him completely. About Jesus, many people say, "I believe!" But they haven't put their full trust in Christ's finished work: His dying for our sins, being buried and rising again on the third day.

Consider this: Blondin walking over Niagara Falls can illustrate an important truth. What if a shoreline disaster meant that the only way to safety was to trust Blondin and to get into his wheelbarrow? Jesus Christ, by the power of His cross, has become the bridge for you to escape the flames of the Lake of Fire. Will you trust Him completely to carry you to the other side? Or will you just mouth the words, "I believe" and avoid getting into the wheelbarrow of His great grace? This is known as receiving the grace of God in vain. This is why the apostle Paul wrote, "*We then, as workers together with Him, beseech you also that ye receive not the grace of God in vain . . . behold, now is the accepted time; behold, now is the day of salvation.*"[93] Don't *twist* the grace of God to use it in vain. Don't *try to comply* by doing your best to cross the separation between God and you. *Trust* what Jesus, your Substitute and Savior, has done for you. Place your complete dependence on Jesus Christ and His finished work today.

Remember: those three witnesses are inviting you to begin your conversations with the Lord. God's creation surrounds you and says to you that God is glorious. Your conscience is also testifying within you to remind you about your rebellion against this glorious God. And the Comforter, the Holy Spirit, who has warned you, is welcoming you into a conversation with the Lord. Are you ready to start?

---

[93] 2 Corinthians 6:1–2

You Need to Have a Conversation with the Lord

Early in this book, we set out to answer the question, "Why? Why am I here? And why are things so messed up in this world? Why can't I find real meaning in life?" Using the word G.R.A.C.E. we have learned what the Bible says about "Why?" God created mankind and crowned him with royal glory and honor, to reflect His unique excellence. But now, men and women everywhere are searching for that meaning, sensing that it has been lost. Why was it lost? Sin, the rebellion of man against the glory of God, brought us under the curse and in bondage to the fear of death. But Christ paid the penalty for the sins of mankind for all those who would embrace Him by faith. So now it's time for you to have your conversation with the Lord.

Listening in on Others' Conversations

One of the most fascinating aspects of God's Word of grace is the number of conversations it contains. The Lord included soul-searching conversations in His Word so that we could listen in. As you read them, they will teach you how to have your own conversation with God.

Jesus even taught us a parable about how each of us could have a life-changing conversation with the Lord. Would you like to read it? It's based on His experience of ministering to rebellious mankind. This parable is found in the Gospel of Luke, chapter 18, and it is included below. As you read it, think about the very different conversations that these two men had with God:

Two men went up into the temple to pray; the one a
Pharisee, and the other a publican [tax collector]. The
Pharisee stood and prayed thus with himself, God, I thank
thee, that I am not as other men are, extortioners, unjust,
adulterers, or even as this publican. I fast twice in the week,
I give tithes of all that I possess.

And the publican, standing afar off, would not lift up so
much as his eyes unto heaven, but smote upon his breast,
saying, "God be merciful to me a sinner."

I tell you, this man went down to his house justified rather than
the other: for every one that exalteth himself shall be abased;
and he that humbleth himself shall be exalted. (Luke 18:10–14)

With shallow thanks, the Pharisee silently spoke to God, but his proud heart proclaimed his personal righteousness. He did not trust God; he believed that he had what it took to please God. That Pharisee not only *twisted* what God had said about man's righteousness, he also *tried to comply* by fasting, giving and doing good things. So he thought of himself as superior to the sinful tax collector.

But the humbled tax collector cried out, *"God, be merciful to me a sinner!"*[94]

Only those who see God's glory clearly are humbled by their poverty of spirit. Using the illustration of the Pharisee and the tax collector, Jesus described well-known classes of people. In that culture, both the Pharisees and tax collectors would have known about the Old Testament sacrifices. They knew about the details of the Temple, including the Ark of the Covenant, which represented the presence of God. The lid of the Ark was also called the "mercy seat."[95] And the word that Jesus used to tell this story points to that mercy seat. In essence, the tax collector prayed, "Lord, be my mercy seat!" or "Be my sacrifice!"

---

[94] This is an excerpt from my book, *12 Ways You Can Make a Difference in This Crazy, Mixed-up World*. It's included in the chapter entitled "Poor in Spirit." Becoming poor in spirit is the first essential way to make a difference.
[95] See Hebrews 9:5

And Jesus testified that, from that moment, the tax collector went down to his house as a man whom God had declared to be righteous in His sight! But the other man continued in his self-righteous, self-exalting ways. Be warned: the highway to Heaven is hidden in humility but the path to punishment is paved with pride.

In His parable, Jesus showed repentant rebels how to humbly approach the glorious God. Across the ages, more than one sinner has entered into everlasting life by beginning the conversation with the words, *"God, be merciful to me a sinner!"*

Nearly thirty years ago a man sat in my office and said to me, "Well, I had my little talk with the Lord this week."

"That's wonderful," I said, "What did you talk to Him about?"

He responded, "Well, I told Him that I was a sinner and that I needed to be saved. I asked Him to save me and He did!"

It was my great joy to watch the Lord transform that man's life and I am convinced the Lord can do the same thing for you.

My Religion Almost Stood in My Way

Perhaps you are just like me when I had a conversation with a counselor on the evening of December 28, 1971. Deeply moved by what I was hearing about the glories of God and my rebellion against Him, I sought out a counselor after an evening service at camp. As we talked, he shared Bible verses with me.

As he listened, I insisted, "I've just got to be a Christian! I prayed that prayer that a teacher led me through when I was eight years old."

"Then why are you sitting here?" he asked.

"That's what I'm trying to figure out!" I exclaimed, "I go to church. I memorize Bible verses. I do the things that religious people are supposed to do. So I've just got to be a Christian!"

Throughout our discussion that evening, the counselor patiently repeated, "So, why are you sitting here?"

The preaching of God's Word at that camp had unveiled my self-deceptive secrets and my conscience would not let me *twist* the truth or *try to comply* any more. My long conversation with that counselor ended well into the night without me finding any rest for my soul. But the next night, sitting in my chair during a fireside service, I placed all my faith in Christ. I called out to Jesus from my heart and said, "Lord, I'm all yours!" I knew that Christ had died for my sins and that God the Father had raised Him from the dead, and I called upon Jesus as Lord. Rather than *twist* or *try* any more, I chose to *trust* Him. That was the beginning of a radical transformation in my life. I know from experience that the Lord can change your life in the same way.

Don't Let Religion Stand in Your Way

There is an interesting story in the Bible about a man who wanted to have this conversation with God, but he didn't know how. Cornelius was a devout military man who lived in Israel at Caesarea on the coast of the Mediterranean. Acts 10:2 tells us that he was *"A devout man, and one that feared God with all his house, which gave much alms to the people, and prayed to God always."*

"Now," you might say, "I think that man, Cornelius, already had a relationship with God and conversed with Him. After all, he was so religious."

But a highly unusual occurrence tells us otherwise. While the Bible was still being written, God sent an angel to Cornelius to tell him to send for the Apostle Peter who was in the nearby town of Joppa. His men found Peter and he agreed to travel with them to meet with Cornelius. The results of that meeting in Caesarea were absolutely amazing, filled with good news of great joy.[96] But we need to answer that question: If Cornelius was trying to talk to God, didn't he have a relationship with God?

---

[96] You can read this fascinating story in Acts 10.

You can see why this question is so important to religious people throughout the world. Many are trying to pray and even giving money to help the poor. But when Peter reported the events in Caesarea to his church in Jerusalem, a startling fact came out.[97] The angel had told Cornelius something important about Peter. The angel told Cornelius to find *"Peter, who shall tell thee words, whereby thou and all thy house shall be saved."*[98] In other words, Cornelius did not have a saving relationship with God. But Peter would deliver the message of salvation by which Cornelius could have such a relationship. What was that message? It was the gospel of grace, and it's the same way you can have that relationship with God and fellowship with Him forever.

How did Peter begin that gospel message to Cornelius and those gathered with him? He began by glorifying God. He noted that the glorious God is impartial, earnestly appealing to all the nations. He is the God who has promised to embrace those who trust Him. You probably know religious people who need to hear this story and this message. In fact, you may be such a person. Well, here is the good news. Peter proclaimed to Cornelius that Jesus Christ was slain on a cross but that God raised Him up three days later.

"Now," you might be saying, "I know that story." But here is an important question: do you know the significance of that story?"

Peter explained, *"To Him give all the prophets witness, that through His name whosoever believeth in Him shall receive remission [forgiveness] of sins"*[99]

Peter emphasized that God had filled the Bible with prophecies and promises about Christ that Cornelius and his men should embrace by faith. They did and you should too.

God has completed the Word of His grace by inspiring His very words in its pages. So now you don't need an angel to startle you with a message; the Lord has given you everything you need to do

---

[97] You can read this report in Acts 11.   [98] Acts 11:13–14   [99] Acts 10:43

His will. In fact, if the angels of heaven could speak to you right now, they would say, "Find someone who can give you the good news of salvation in Christ found in the Bible!" That is what this book is about. Don't let religious rituals and deeds stand between you and a saving relationship with the Lord. Embrace Him by faith and enjoy talking to Him!

Don't Clench Your Fists and Walk Away

Years ago, I led a jail ministry in Tarboro, North Carolina. My team and I had wonderful times sharing the good news of grace as we talked to the prisoners there. But one day I found out that there was a man in solitary who was so vile that even the jailers would not talk to him. Intrigued, I began to visit the man each week and soon discovered that I was the only person who would talk to him. I could tell that he welcomed my visits, but he often began to verbally attack me as soon as I came within sight.

"Here he is," he mocked, "the man who believes in the triple god: God the Father, God the Son and God the Holy Spirit."

He insisted that his religion taught otherwise. As I prayed for this man, the Lord gave me the wisdom to ask him an important question one day.

I said, "Please tell me about your god. Is he just? Does he give you exactly what you deserve?"

"Oh, yes!" he exclaimed, "He is just and gives me exactly what I deserve."

"So," I inquired, "what about the evil in your life? Does he forgive you?"

"Yes," he smiled, "He does forgive me."

"Well, this is what I don't understand," I continued, "how can he be just, giving you exactly what you deserve, and yet forgive you, which, almost by definition, is not giving you what you deserve? I don't understand that. Could you explain it to me?"

He pondered the matter for a few moments. I could tell by the movement of his hands that he was going back and forth in his thoughts.

Finally, he looked at me and asked, "What do you believe?"

I responded, "I believe that God the Father sent God the Son to this earth to live the righteous life that I should have lived. But then, God the Son was willing to be put to death on the cross of Calvary as my substitute. God the Father poured out everything that I deserved on Him. Only on that basis can the Father forgive me because the penalty for my rebellion is completely paid."

His eyes widened as he grasped the truth of God's great grace. But after a moment, he screwed his eyes shut and clenched his fists as he screamed, "Get away from me! Get away from me!"

Don't be like that prisoner. When you see the glory of God and His grace for mankind, then embrace Christ by faith. Since Christ paid the penalty, no man needs to try to pay it himself; he can trust what Jesus did. This remarkable plan leads to no contradiction within the true and living God. As the apostle wrote about God, *"To declare, I say, at this time His righteousness: that He might be just, and the justifier of him which believeth in Jesus."* [100] There is no contradiction: God is just and He forgives repentant rebels because of what Jesus did for us.

Mixing Your Faith with God's Promises

Years ago, the parents of a dying girl asked me to talk to their young daughter. She was troubled about whether or not she was really going to Heaven. She needed rest for her soul.

As I sat by her bedside I asked, "Have you ever baked a cake with your mommy?"

"Yes," she said and smiled at the memory of the many times she had helped her mother in the kitchen.

---

[100] Romans 3:26

"What did you do when you made that cake?" I asked.

She told me about all the ingredients and how they would mix them together to make delicious cakes.

"Have you ever mixed concrete with your father?" I inquired. (Her father is a contractor.)

"Yes!" she said.

"Do you remember?" her father chimed in, "You even placed your handprint in the concrete we poured for the garage!"

"That's right" she grinned, clearly enjoying that memory as well.

"Now this is what I want to show you," I continued. "This is how you find rest for your soul. In Hebrews 4:1–2, the Bible says, *"Let us therefore fear, lest a promise being left us of entering into His rest, any of you should seem to come short of it. For unto us was the gospel preached, as well as unto them: but the Word preached did not profit them, not being mixed with faith in them that heard it."* This is how you find rest for your soul. Just like you helped your mommy make those cake mixes, and helped your daddy mix concrete, you have to mix something together."

"What do I need to mix together?" she asked, a little puzzled.

"Those verses say that you need to mix your faith with the promises of God," I replied, "that is how you find rest for your soul."

"I see," she replied.

I continued, "And just like you mixed that concrete and it set up to form a foundation that you can park your car on, it's the same way for your soul. If you mix your faith with God's promises of salvation, you will have a sure foundation. Do you understand?"

"Yes," she said excitedly.

"So," I asked, "which promises of God can you tell me about?"

She smiled as she quoted John 3:16 and many of the other Bible promises that are included in this book. That night, she gained the complete assurance that she was on her way to Heaven by mixing her faith with those promises. Now will you mix your faith with the promises of God?

Today Is the Day of Salvation

If someone gave you this book, this is why. They loved you enough to work together with the Lord to be sure that you learn the message of the Gospel. As you have read this book, God has been showing you His gracious favor. Don't receive this grace in vain. Now is the accepted time. Today is the day of salvation. Why not begin your conversation with the Lord right now?

Glorify God by praising Him for His wonders. Then confess your rebellion against God by humbly crying out, "God be merciful to me a sinner!" Then, if you believe that Christ died for your sins, was buried and rose again the third day, confess Him as your Lord. I prayed, "Lord, I'm all yours!" If you will place your faith in what Jesus has done for sinners, He will save you. You too will be a participant in the great exchange. Don't *twist*; don't *try*; just *trust*.

Now You Know Why

We started out this book with the question, "Why?" and we have found many Biblical answers. Now we understand why things have been in such a mess throughout the world: it's the rebellion of man along with the awful consequences. But for all who will humbly repent and trust Him, Jesus Christ takes those consequences and gives the humble believer eternal life. If you have found your "Why?" then you have found your way. Jesus Christ said, *"I am the way, the truth, the life, no man cometh unto the Father but by me."* [101]

People Love You

God loves you and those who have trusted Him also love you. It may be that one of them gave you this book. When you are ready, it would be important to tell that person what has happened in your life. He or she can help you find a good church where this gospel message is proclaimed and explained. If you have no one to help you and you need to reach me to talk further, I would be glad to correspond with you. You can contact me through my website at www.LiveServeLead.com.

---

[101] John 14:6

To reorder, please visit LiveServeLead.com
"Live, serve, lead, helping others succeed"

Other books by Gordon A. Dickson
12 Ways You Can Make a Difference
in This Crazy, Mixed-up World

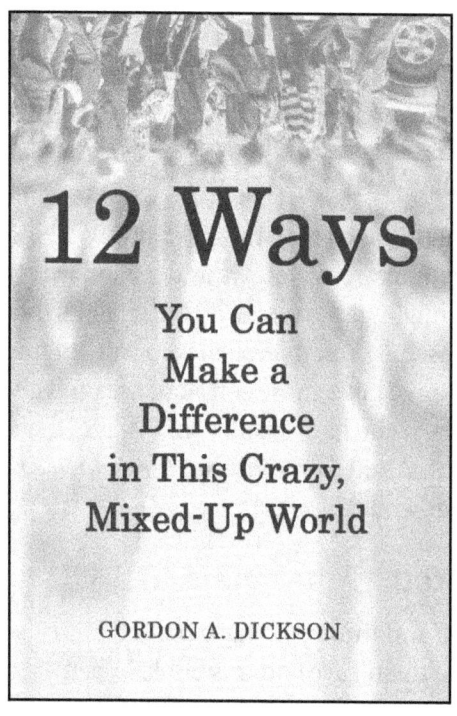

www.ingramcontent.com/pod-product-compliance
Lightning Source LLC
Chambersburg PA
CBHW071721140626
46557CB00012B/1179